HEART

LOVE & GRACE

HEART

Mary Drum (B.Th)

GRACE

INTRODUCTION

Grace is god's own loving kindness and favour toward human beings, given freely so we can respond to his call to become children of God. Grace is participation in the life of God.

HEART: LOVE & GRACE

Love, in the modern world, is a term that has come to mean something romantic. Yet the full meaning and history of love concerns far more than romantic or even conjugal love. Saint Paul speaks of *agape:* a Greek word for love that encompasses charity. The value of this particular word is that it describes something common and known to us all in the love relationships of family and friends but also, in faith, reflects the mystery of something ultimately indescribable.

The love being explored in this book is the love of the greatest commandment: "to love one another as I have loved you." The simple word "as" represents all that Jesus taught and lived. It is an almost inconceivable goal to love one another as Jesus loved us, and yet we are to try to do so. On the cross Jesus said to his Father – and our Father: "Forgive them for they know not what they do". From this I take hope that I will be forgiven for the times that I fail to love because I know that I am unconditionally loved by God. Here the human experience of love meets God's loving grace.

The Christian Church is a pilgrim Church sustained by and through love. As pilgrim companions on the journey we love the sinner and the saint as Jesus did and still does.

1Co 13:1-13

HEART: LOVE & GRACE

1 CORINTHIANS 13:1-13

If I speak in the tongues of men and of angels, but have not love, I am only a resounding gong or a clanging cymbal. If I have the gift of prophecy and can fathom all mysteries and all knowledge, and if I have a faith that can move mountains, but have not love, I am nothing. If I give all I possess to the poor and surrender my body to the flames but have not love, I gain nothing. Love is patient, love is kind. It does not envy, it does not boast, it is not proud. It is not rude, it is not self-seeking, it is not easily angered, it keeps no record of wrongs. Love does not delight in evil but rejoices with the truth. It always protects, always trusts, always hopes, always perseveres. Love never fails. But where there are prophecies, they will cease; where there are tongues, they will be stilled; where there is knowledge, it will pass away. For we know in part and we prophesy in part, but when perfection comes, the imperfect disappears. When I was a child, I talked like a child, I thought like a child, I reasoned like a child. When I became a man, I put childish ways behind me. Now we see but a poor reflection as in a mirror; then we shall see face to face. Now I know in part; then I shall know fully, even as I am fully known. And now these three remain: faith, hope and love. But the greatest of these is love.

CREATION

By grace, creation is the greatest gift of love.

GE 1:1-2

GENESIS 1:1-2

In the beginning God created
the heavens and the earth.
Now the earth was formless
and empty, darkness was over
the surface of the deep, and
the Spirit of God was hovering
over the waters.

GENESIS 1:3-5
And God said, "Let there be
light," and there was light.

God saw that the light was
good, and he separated the
light from the darkness.

God called the light "day,"
and the darkness he called
"night." And there was
evening, and there was
morning – the first day.

GE 1:6-14

And God said, "Let there be an expanse between the waters to separate water from water."

So God made the expanse and separated the water under the expanse from the water above it. And it was so.

God called the expanse "sky." And there was evening, and there was morning – the second day.

And God said, "Let the water under the sky be gathered to one place, and let dry ground appear." And it was so.

God called the dry ground "land," and the gathered waters he called "seas." And God saw that it was good.

Then God said, "Let the land produce vegetation: seed-bearing plants and trees on the land that bear fruit with seed in it, according to their various kinds." And it was so.

The land produced vegetation: plants bearing seed according to their kinds and trees bearing fruit with seed in it according to their kinds. And God saw that it was good.

And there was evening, and there was morning – the third day.

And God said, "Let there be lights in the expanse of the sky to separate the day from the night, and let them serve as signs to mark seasons and days and years."

GENESIS 1:16-21

God made two great lights – the greater light to govern the day and the lesser light to govern the night. He also made the stars. God set them in the expanse of the sky to give light on the earth, to govern the day and the night, and to separate light from darkness. And God saw that it was good. And there was evening, and there was morning – the fourth day. And God said, "Let the water teem with living creatures, and let birds fly above the earth across the expanse of the sky." So God created the great creatures of the sea and every living and moving thing.

GENESIS 1:24-25

And God said, "Let the land produce living creatures according to their kinds: livestock, creatures that move along the ground, and wild animals, each according to its kind." And it was so.

God made the wild animals according to their kinds, the livestock according to their kinds, and all the creatures that move along the ground according to their kinds. And God saw that it was good.

GENESIS 1:26-28

Then God said, "Let us make
man in our image, in our
likeness, and let them rule over
the fish of the sea and the
birds of the air, over the
livestock, over all the earth,
and over all the creatures that
move along the ground."

So God created man in his
own image, in the image of
God he created him; male
and female he created them.

God blessed them and said
to them, "Be fruitful and
increase in number; fill the
earth and subdue it. Rule over
the fish of the sea and the
birds of the air and over every
living creature that moves on
the ground."

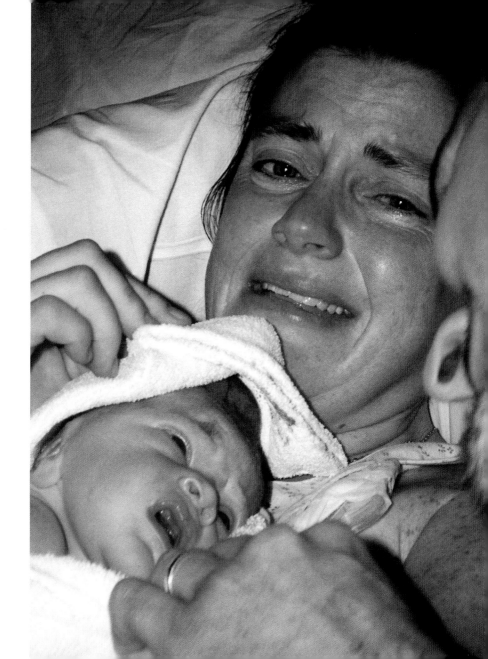

EXODUS 15:11
Who among the gods is like
you, O LORD?
Who is like you – majestic in
holiness, awesome in glory,
working wonders?

Ex 15:11

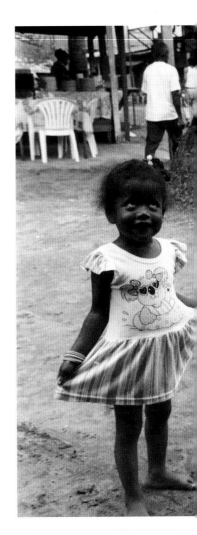

SIRACH 17:11-12
He bestowed knowledge
upon them, and alloted to
them the law of life,

He established with them
an eternal covenant, and
revealed to them his decrees.

JOHN 1:1-5
In the beginning was the
Word, and the Word was with
God, and the Word was God.
He was with God in the
beginning. Through him all
things were made; without him
nothing was made that has
been made. In him was life,
and that life was the light of
men. The light shines in the
darkness, but the darkness has
not understood it.

JN 1:1-5

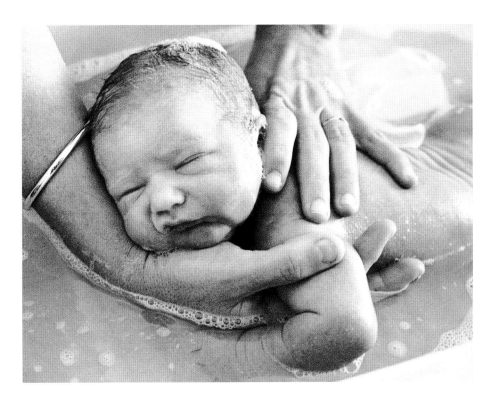

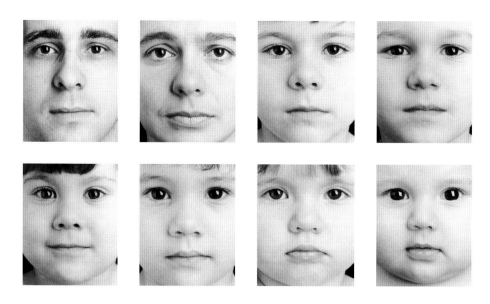

Ps 8:3-4

PSALM 8:3-4
When I consider your heavens,
the work of your fingers, the
moon and the stars, which you
have set in place, what is man
that you are mindful of him,
the son of man that you care
for him?

REVELATION 4:11
"You are worthy, our Lord and
God, to receive glory and
honour and power, for you
created all things, and by your
will they were created and
have their being."

RE 4:11

LOVE

Created and Creator are in covenant with each other. Love is a caring commitment in which we show affection for, and delight in, others. This love is grounded in the nature of God himself and in the life of Jesus – through his words and actions, and, supremely, in his death on the cross. God demonstrates the nature of love and defines the direction in which human love in all its forms should take.

MATTHEW 22:37-40
Jesus replied: "'Love the Lord
your God with all your heart
and with all your soul and with
all your mind.'

This is the first and greatest
commandment.

And the second is like it: 'Love
your neighbour as yourself.'

All the Law and the Prophets
hang on these two
commandments."

1 JOHN 4:10

This is love: not that we loved
God, but that he loved us and
sent his Son as an atoning
sacrifice for our sins.

MK 12:30-31

JOHN 15:15
I no longer call you servants,
because a servant does not
know his master's business.
Instead, I have called you
friends, for everything that I
learned from my Father I have
made known to you.

JOHN 19:26-27

When Jesus saw his mother there, and the disciple whom he loved standing nearby, he said to his mother, "Dear woman, here is your son," and to the disciple, "Here is your mother." From that time on, this disciple took her into his home.

1 JOHN 4:7-8
Dear friends, let us love one another, for love comes from God. Everyone who loves has been born of God and knows God.

Whoever does not love does not know God, because God is love.

GALATIANS 5:22-23
But the fruit of the Spirit is love,
joy, peace, patience, kindness,
goodness, faithfulness,
gentleness and self-control
and against such things there
is no law.

JOHN 13:35
"By this all men will know that
you are my disciples, if you
love one another."

Ps 23:1-6

PSALM 23:1-6
The LORD is my shepherd,
I shall not be in want.

He makes me lie down in
green pastures, he leads me
beside quiet waters,

he restores my soul. He guides
me in paths of righteousness
for his name's sake.

Even though I walk through
the valley of the shadow of
death, I will fear no evil, for you
are with me; your rod and
your staff, they comfort me.

You prepare a table before
me in the presence of my
enemies. You anoint my head
with oil; my cup overflows.

Surely goodness and love will
follow me all the days of my
life, and I will dwell in the
house of the LORD forever.

PSALM 36:9-10
For with you is the fountain of
life; in your light we see light.
Continue your love to those
who know you, your righteousness to the upright in heart.

CHARITY

JOHN 15:9-10 "As the Father has loved me, so have I loved you. Now remain in my love If you obey my commands, you will remain in my love, just as I have obeyed my Father's commands and remain in his love."

Charity is a particular form of love. It is the virtue that allows us to love God above all else and to love our neighbour as ourselves. We do both these things for the sake of all, including our own sake. In charity "I" and "You" are not opposed to each other but, rather, relate as "We".

DEUTERONOMY 7:8-9

But it was because the LORD
loved you and kept the oath
he swore to your forefathers
that he brought you out with
a mighty hand and redeemed
you from the land of slavery,
from the power of Pharaoh
king of Egypt.

Know therefore that the
LORD your God is God; he is
the faithful God, keeping his
covenant of love to a
thousand generations of
those who love him and
keep his commands.

JOHN 15:16
You did not choose me, but I
chose you and appointed you
to go and bear fruit – fruit that
will last. Then the Father will
give you whatever you ask in
my name.

1 JOHN 4:21

And he has given us this command: Whoever loves God must also love his brother.

Love must be sincere. Hate what is evil; cling to what is good.

Be devoted to one another in brotherly love. Honour one another above yourselves.

Never be lacking in zeal, but keep your spiritual fervour, serving the Lord.

Be joyful in hope, patient in affliction, faithful in prayer.

Share with God's people who are in need. Practice hospitality.

Bless those who persecute you; bless and do not curse.

Rejoice with those who rejoice; mourn with those who mourn.

Live in harmony with one another. Do not be proud, but be willing to associate with people of low position. Do not be conceited.

Do not repay anyone evil for evil. Be careful to do what is right in the eyes of everybody.

If it is possible, as far as it depends on you, live at peace with everyone.

Do not take revenge, my friends, but leave room for God's wrath, for it is written: "It is mine to avenge; I will repay," says the Lord.

On the contrary: "If your enemy is hungry, feed him; if he is thirsty, give him something to drink. In doing this, you will heap burning coals on his head."

Do not be overcome by evil, but overcome evil with good.

Be on your guard; stand firm in the faith; be men of courage; be strong.

Do everything in love.

1 CORINTHIANS 16:13-14

MATTHEW 10:40
"He who receives you receives
me, and he who receives me
receives the one who sent me."

PHILIPPIANS 2:1-3

If you have any
encouragement from being
united with Christ, if any
comfort from his love, if any
fellowship with the Spirit, if any
tenderness and compassion,

then make my joy complete
by being like-minded, having
the same love, being one in
spirit and purpose.

Do nothing out of selfish
ambition or vain conceit, but
in humility consider others
better than yourselves.

LUKE 14:16-24

Jesus replied: "A certain man was preparing a great banquet and invited many guests.

At the time of the banquet he sent his servant to tell those who had been invited, 'Come, for everything is now ready.'

But they all alike began to make excuses. The first said, 'I have just bought a field, and I must go and see it. Please excuse me.'

Another said, 'I have just bought five yoke of oxen, and I'm on my way to try them out. Please excuse me.'

Still another said, 'I just got married, so I can't come.'

The servant came back and reported this to his master. Then the owner of the house became angry and ordered his servant, 'Go out quickly into the streets and alleys of the town and bring in the poor, the crippled, the blind and the lame.'

'Sir,' the servant said, 'what you ordered has been done, but there is still room.'

Then the master told his servant, 'Go out to the roads and country lanes and make them come in, so that my house will be full. I tell you, not one of those men who were invited will get a taste of my banquet.'"

LUKE 10:25-37

On one occasion an expert in the law stood up to test Jesus. "Teacher," he asked, "what must I do to inherit eternal life?"

"What is written in the Law?" he replied. "How do you read it?"

He answered: "'Love the Lord your God with all your heart and with all your soul and with all your strength and with all your mind'; and, 'Love your neighbour as yourself.'

"You have answered correctly," Jesus replied. "Do this and you will live."

But he wanted to justify himself, so he asked Jesus, "And who is my neighbour?"

In reply Jesus said: "A man was going down from Jerusalem to Jericho, when he fell into the hands of robbers. They stripped him of his clothes, beat him and went away, leaving him half dead.

"A priest happened to be going down the same road, and when he saw the man, he passed by on the other side. So too, a Levite, when he came to the place and saw him, passed by on the other side.

"But a Samaritan, as he traveled, came where the man was; and when he saw him, he took pity on him.

"He went to him and bandaged his wounds, pouring on oil and wine. Then he put the man on his own donkey, took him to an inn and took care of him.

"The next day he took out two silver coins and gave them to the innkeeper. 'Look after him,' he said, 'and when I return, I will reimburse you for any extra expense you may have.'

"Which of these three do you think was a neighbour to the man who fell into the hands of robbers?"

The expert in the law replied, "The one who had mercy on him." Jesus told him, "Go and do likewise."

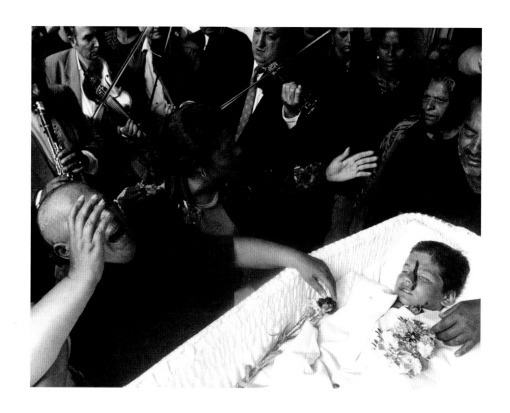

Romans 2:6-7
God "will give to each person
according to what he has
done." To those who by
persistence in doing good
seek glory, honour and
immortality, he will give eternal
life.

MATTHEW 6:1-4

"Be careful not to do your 'acts of righteousness' before men, to be seen by them. If you do, you will have no reward from your Father in heaven.

"So when you give to the needy, do not announce it with trumpets, as the hypocrites do in the synagogues and on the streets, to be honoured by men. I tell you the truth, they have received their reward in full.

But when you give to the needy, do not let your left hand know what your right hand is doing, so that your giving may be in secret. Then your Father, who sees what is done in secret, will reward you."

ROMANS 15:1-3
We who are strong ought to
bear with the failings of the
weak and not to please
ourselves.

Each of us should please his
neighbour for his good, to
build him up.

For even Christ did not please
himself but, as it is written: "The
insults of those who insult you
have fallen on me."

MISSION

ROMANS 8:14 Because those who are led by the Spirit of God are sons of God.

ACTS 1:8 "But you will receive power when the Holy Spirit comes on you; and you will be my witnesses in Jerusalem, and in all Judea and Samaria, and to the ends of the earth."

If we love and are no longer isolated as "I" and "You", together we relate as "We".

"We" means that we have a mission to be Jesus to each other in the love of the Holy Spirit. Jesus showed how this is possible in his love for the Father and for others. The mission is the "as" in his second commandment. It is here that we can meet the Spirit and recognise our own charisms. As the apostles went forth, so too must we also who believe in Jesus Christ.

Our pilgrim Church continues on mission to the world. While I cannot expect that the world would turn Christian during my time on Earth and while I can thank God for the rich religious traditions in the world, nevertheless, the Church hopes the world will come somehow to recognise Christ.

In all the years of my study, one of the most difficult tasks given me has involved inter-religious dialogue. I have learned how people of other faiths interpret the practices of Christians which seem at odds with what people expect of us.

When we say we are Christian we must work in concert with the Holy Spirit; and this requires strength in our faith to continue on mission in our pluralist world. Jesus Christ is our saviour; it is his mission of love to which we are called to be apostles.

ROMANS 12:1-8

Therefore, I urge you, brothers, in view of God's mercy, to offer your bodies as living sacrifices, holy and pleasing to God – this is your spiritual act of worship.

Do not conform any longer to the pattern of this world, but be transformed by the renewing of your mind. Then you will be able to test and

of faith God has given you. Just as each of us has one body with many members, and these members do not all have the same function, so in Christ we who are many form one body, and each member belongs to all the others.

We have different gifts, according to the grace given us. If a man's gift is

RO 12:1-8

approve what God's will is – his good, pleasing and perfect will.

For by the grace given me I say to every one of you: Do not think of yourself more highly than you ought, but rather think of yourself with sober judgment, in accordance with the measure

prophesying, let him use it in proportion to his faith.
If it is serving, let him serve; if it is teaching, let him teach; if it is encouraging, let him encourage; if it is contributing to the needs of others, let him give generously; if it is leadership, let him govern diligently; if it is showing mercy, let him do it cheerfully.

ACTS 6:5-10

This proposal pleased the
whole group. They chose
Stephen, a man full of faith
and of the Holy Spirit; also
Philip, Procorus, Nicanor, Timon,
Parmenas, and
Nicolas from Antioch, a
convert to Judaism.

They presented these men to
the apostles, who prayed
and laid their hands on them.

So the word of God spread.
The number of disciples in
Jerusalem increased rapidly,
and a large number of priests
became obedient to the faith.
Now Stephen, a man full of
God's grace and power, did
great wonders and miraculous
signs among the people.

Opposition arose, however,
from members of the
Synagogue of the Freedmen
(as it was called) – Jews of
Cyrene and Alexandria as well
as the provinces of Cilicia
and Asia. These men began to
argue with Stephen but they
could not stand up against his
wisdom or the Spirit by whom
he spoke.

1 THESSALONIANS 2:7-8

As apostles of Christ we could have been a burden to you, but we were gentle among you, like a mother caring for her little children.

We loved you so much that we were delighted to share with you not only the gospel of God but our lives as well, because you had become so dear to us.

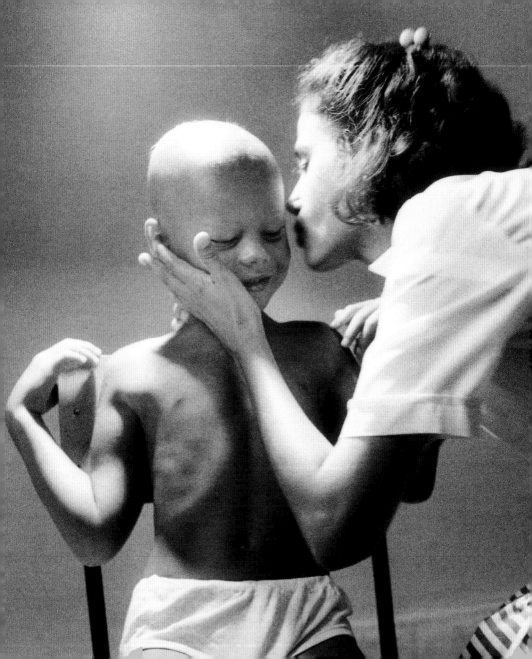

1 PETER 4:19
So then, those who suffer according to God's will should commit themselves to their faithful Creator and continue to do good.

ROMANS 8:28
And we know that in all things God works for the good of those who love him, who have been called according to his purpose.

JEREMIAH 17:8
"He will be like a tree planted
by the water that sends out its
roots by the stream. It does not
fear when heat comes; its
leaves are always green. It has
no worries in a year of drought
and never fails to bear fruit."

RO 13:8-10

ROMANS 13:8-10

Let no debt remain outstanding, except the continuing debt to love one another, for he who loves his fellowman has fulfilled the law.

The commandments, "Do not commit adultery," "Do not murder," "Do not steal," "Do not covet," and whatever other commandment there may be, are summed up in this one rule:

"Love your neighbour as yourself." Love does no harm to its neighbour. Therefore love is the fulfillment of the law.

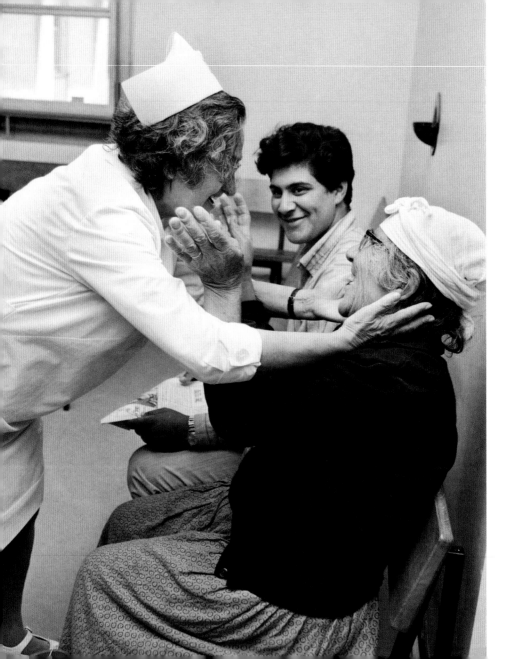

EPHESIANS 6:10-20
Finally, be strong in the Lord and in his mighty power.

Put on the full armour of God so that you can take your stand against the devil's schemes.

For our struggle is not against flesh and blood, but against the rulers, against the authorities, against the powers of this dark world and against the spiritual forces of evil in the heavenly realms.

Therefore put on the full armour of God, so that when the day of evil comes, you may be able to stand your ground, and after you have done everything, to stand.

Stand firm then, with the belt of truth buckled around your waist, with the breastplate of righteousness in place, and with your feet fitted with the readiness that comes from the gospel of peace.

In addition to all this, take up the shield of faith, with which you can extinguish all the flaming arrows of the evil one.

Take the helmet of salvation and the sword of the Spirit, which is the word of God.

And pray in the Spirit on all occasions with all kinds of prayers and requests. With this in mind, be alert and always keep on praying for all the saints.

Pray also for me, that whenever I open my mouth, words may be given me so that I will fearlessly make known the mystery of the gospel, for which I am an ambassador in chains. Pray that I may declare it fearlessly, as I should.

EPH 6:10-20

MATTHEW 10:5-6
These twelve Jesus sent out with the following instructions: "Do not go among the Gentiles or enter any town of the Samaritans. Go rather to the lost sheep of Israel."

PSALM 34:1 I will extol the LORD at all times;
his praise will always be on my lips.

STRANGER

Jesus knows first hand what it is like to be a stranger. As a very young child, he had been exiled in Egypt, as had the tribes of Jewish tradition.

Jesus teaches us to be inclusive and that there is no such thing as the stranger if we love one another as he has loved us. It may be hard to share the gospel with people of other nations and faiths – with people who seem strange to us. It can be easier to fear than to love. Yet love will bring rich rewards. There is nothing to fear but fear itself; and the stranger in need gives us an opportunity to show how deeply we can love even others with whom we have had no prior connection, apart from the fact that we are human persons being created by God.

EXODUS 23:9
Do not oppress an alien; you
yourselves know how it feels to
be aliens, because you were
aliens in Egypt.

DEUTERONOMY 10:17-18
For the LORD your God is God
of gods and Lord of lords, the
great God, mighty and
awesome, who shows no
partiality and accepts no
bribes. He defends the cause
of the fatherless and the
widow, and loves the alien,
giving him food and clothing.

Ezra 10:44
All these had married foreign
women, and some of them
had children by these wives.

LEV 19:9-10

LEVITICUS 19:9-10

When you reap the harvest of
your land, do not reap to the
very edges of your field or
gather the gleanings of your
harvest.

Do not go over your vineyard
a second time or pick up the
grapes that have fallen.
Leave them for the poor and
the alien. I am the LORD
your God.

EXODUS 12:49
The same law applies to the
native-born and to the alien
living among you.

LEVITICUS 19:33
When an alien lives with you in
your land, do not mistreat him.

HEBREWS 13:1-2
Keep on loving each other
as brothers.

Do not forget to entertain
strangers, for by so doing some
people have entertained
angels without knowing it.

GALATIANS 3:26-28
You are all sons of God
through faith in Christ Jesus,

for all of you who were
baptised into Christ have
clothed yourselves with Christ.

There is neither Jew nor Greek,
slave nor free, male nor
female, for you are all one in
Christ Jesus.

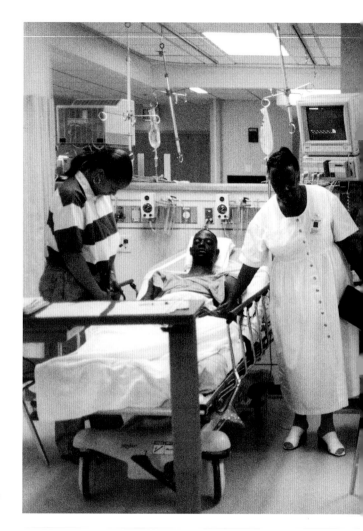

LUKE 17:11-19
Now on his way to Jerusalem,
Jesus traveled along the
border between Samaria and
Galilee.

As he was going into a village,
ten men who had leprosy met
him. They stood at a distance
and called out in a loud
voice, "Jesus, Master, have pity
on us!"

When he saw them, he said,
"Go, show yourselves to the
priests." And as they went, they
were cleansed.

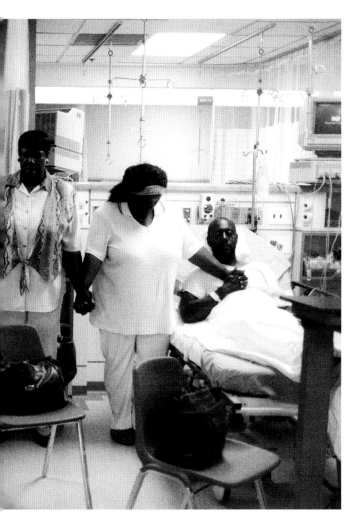

One of them, when he saw he was healed, came back, praising God in a loud voice.

He threw himself at Jesus' feet and thanked him – and he was a Samaritan.

Jesus asked, "Were not all ten cleansed? Where are the other nine?

Was no one found to return and give praise to God except this foreigner?"

Then he said to him, "Rise and go; your faith has made you well."

JUSTICE

Since we are all created as persons equal in dignity, justice is paramount. It is a cardinal virtue that must be a constant in our love of others.

Justice and wisdom come together. By tuning in to the wisdom of God, we can love as the Father and Jesus do. We can be just.

1 Corinthians 4:1-2

So then, men ought to regard us as servants of Christ and as those entrusted with the secret things of God.

Now it is required that those who have been given a trust must prove faithful.

Psalm 37:25-26
I was young and now I am
old, yet I have never seen the
righteous forsaken or their
children begging bread.

They are always generous and
lend freely; their children will
be blessed.

127

1 PETER 4:8-9
Above all, love each other
deeply, because love covers
over a multitude of sins.

Offer hospitality to one
another without grumbling.

PSALM 33:5
The LORD loves righteousness
and justice; the earth is full of
his unfailing love.

DEUTERONOMY 24:14
"Do not take advantage of a
hired man who is poor and
needy, whether he is a brother
Israelite or an alien living in
one of your towns."

EXODUS 22:25
"If you lend money to one of
my people among you who is
needy, do not be like a
moneylender; charge him no
interest."

DEUTERONOMY 10:17

For the LORD your God is God
of gods and Lord of lords,
the great God, mighty and
awesome, who shows no
partiality and accepts
no bribes.

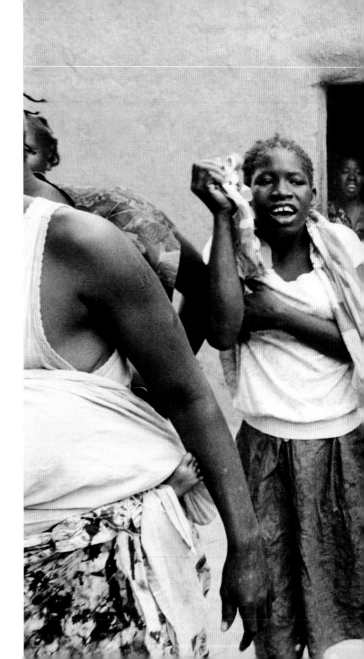

PSALM 34:6
This poor man called, and the
LORD heard him; he saved
him out of all his troubles.

EXODUS 23:1-8

"Do not spread false reports. Do not help a wicked man by being a malicious witness.

"Do not follow the crowd in doing wrong. When you give testimony in a lawsuit, do not pervert justice by siding with the crowd, and do not show favouritism to a poor man in his lawsuit.

"If you come across your enemy's ox or donkey wandering off, be sure to take it back to him. If you see the donkey of someone who hates you fallen down under its load, do not leave it there; be sure you help him with it.

"Do not deny justice to your poor people in their lawsuits. Have nothing to do with a false charge and do not put an innocent or honest person to death, for I will not acquit the guilty.

"Do not accept a bribe, for a bribe blinds those who see and twists the words of the righteous."

PSALM 37:1-6
Do not fret because of evil men
or be envious of those who do
wrong; for like the grass they will
soon wither, like green plants
they will soon die away. Trust in
the LORD and do good; dwell in
the land and enjoy safe
pasture. Delight yourself in the
LORD and he will give you the
desires of your heart. Commit
your way to the LORD; trust in
him and he will do this: He will
make your righteousness shine
like the dawn, the justice of your
cause like the noonday sun.

Ps 37:1-6

ROMANS 15:5
May the God who gives
endurance and
encouragement give you
a spirit of unity among
yourselves as you follow
Christ Jesus.

ROMANS 15:7
Accept one another, then, just
as Christ accepted you, in
order to bring praise to God.

EPHESIANS 2:14
For he himself is our peace,
who has made the two one
and has destroyed the barrier,
the dividing wall of hostility,

PR 21:3 To do what is right and just is more
acceptable to the LORD than sacrifice.

PSALM 37:23-24
If the LORD delights in a man's
way, he makes his steps firm;
and though he stumble, he will
not fall, for the LORD upholds
him with his hand.

COL 3:12 Therefore, as God's chosen people, holy and dearly loved, clothe yourselves with compassion, kindness, humility, gentleness and patience.

COLOSSIANS 3:13-14
Bear with each other and
forgive whatever grievances
you may have against one
another. Forgive as the Lord
forgave you. And over all
these virtues put on love,
which binds them all together
in perfect unity.

Acknowledgements

All images in *Heart* were originally published by **M • I • L • K**™ Publishing Limited and have been used under licence from **M • I • L • K**™ Licensing Limited, all rights reserved. www.milkphotos.com

The images are Copyright © the individual photographers as follows.

P14 Alvein Damardanto
P16 and cover Ben Law-Viljoen
Pp18-19 Yorghos Kontaxis
P20 Fredé Spencer
P22 Ray Peek
P25 Barbara Judith Exeter
P27 Christel Dhuit
Pp28-29 Martin Rosenthal
P31 Kelvin Patrick
P32 Petra Stepan
P35 and cover George Peirce
P39 and cover Dilip Padhi
Pp40-41 Victor Englebert
P42 and cover Todd Davis
P45 and cover Marianne Thomas
P46 and cover Amelia Panico
P48 James Fassinger
Pp50-51 Gunars Binde
P53 Nicholas Ross
P55 Thomas Patrick Kiernan
P56 Paul Knight

Pp60-61 Herman Krieger
Pp62-63 Lorenz Kienzle
P65 and cover Doreen Hemp
Pp66-67 Minh Qúy
P69 and cover Janice Rubin
P70 Marianne Thomas
P73 David Hancock
P74 Ann Versaen
P77 Tamas Kovacs
P78 and cover Sergey Denisov
Pp80-81 Dmitri Korobeinikov
Pp82-83 Michael Agelopas
P87 Al Lieberman
P89 Robin Sparks Daugherty
P90 Jon Holloway
P92 Ivo Saglietti
Pp94-95 Raymond Field
P96 Robert Lifson
P98 Werner Braun
P101 Felix Bialy
P103 and cover David M Grossman

P107 Amit Bar
Pp108-109 Dô Ãnh Tuấn
P110 Romualdas Požerskis
P113 Katherine Fletcher
P115 and cover Pisit Senanunsakul
P116 Peter Gabriel
Pp118-119 Guy Stubbs
Pp120-121 Jim Witmer
P124 and cover Steve Hotson
Pp126-127 José Caldas
P128 and cover Jeremy Rall
P131 Karen Maini
Pp132-133 Alison Williams
Pp134-135 Jacqueline Parker
P137 Philip Kuruvita
P138 Lloyd Erlick
P140 Marice Cohn Band

Published by St Pauls Publications, PO Box 906, Strathfield NSW 2135 Australia,
www.stpauls.com.au

This edition published in 2007 by St Pauls Publications in association with Drum Publishing Pty
Ltd under license from M.I.L.K. Licensing Ltd. Title and concept Copyright © 2007 Mary
Drum Pty Ltd. The right of Mary Drum to be identified as author of this work has been asserted
by her in accordance with the Copyright, Designs and Patents Act 1988.

Images and artwork Copyright © 2007 M.I.L.K. Licensing Ltd.

British Library Cataloguing Data.
A catalogue record for this book is available from the British Library.

Designed by Carolyn Lewis.
Printed and bound by 1010 Printing International Ltd, China.